138

SEP 24 2008

W9-BSM-073

CHILDRENS
DISCARD
Brighton Memorial Library
2300 Elmwood Avenue
Rochester, NY 14618

The Totally TEA~rific TEA PARTY Book

Teas to taste, treats to bake, and crafts to make from around the world and beyond

Tanya Napier

Photography by Julie Brown

Illustrations by Annie Galvin

BARRON'S

The Totally TEA-rific TEA Party Book
Teas to taste, treats to bake, and crafts to make from around the world and beyond.

First edition for the United States and Canada published exclusively by Barron's Educational Series, Inc. in 2002.

Created and produced by Orange Avenue Publishing, Inc., San Francisco.
© 2002 by Orange Avenue Publishing, Inc.
Illustrations © 2002 by Annie Galvin
Photographs © 2002 by Julie Brown

All rights reserved. No part of this book may be reproduced in any form, by photostat, microfilm, xerography, or any other means, or incorporated into any information retrieval system, electronic or mechanical, without the written permission of the copyright owner.

All inquiries should be addressed to:
Barron's Educational Series, Inc.
250 Wireless Boulevard
Hauppauge, NY 11788
http://www.barronseduc.com

International Standard Book No. 0-7641-5493-1

Library of Congress Catalog Card No. 2001093895

Printed in Singapore

9 8 7 6 5 4 3 2 1

The Totally TEA~rific TEA PARTY Book

What's Brewing?

THE STORY OF TEA

NATIVI~TEA
IN THE BEGINNING...

It all started over 5,000 years ago in China with a wise emperor on a windy day. According to ancient and very tea-stained documents, the Shen Nong, as he was known, was outside having some water boiled for his drinking pleasure. Before he could bring the water to his lips, a leaf blew off a bush and into his cup, turning the beverage a curious shade of brown. The emperor was clearly very thirsty. He took a sip, and then many more, declaring the drink to be tasty and refreshing...

VARIE~TEA
...AND THEN THERE WAS TEA

One leaf floated into instant fame, and we have been drinking tea ever since. Today, more tea is drunk around the world than any other beverage. Whether it is green or black, and sipped hot from a teacup or slurped cold from a tall glass, tea has a way of making people happy. But it's not just the tea itself that's *TEA~rific*. It's all the traditions that go along with it. Tea is grown in forty different countries, and there are just as many customs surrounding the way it is prepared. It is the way we enjoy tea when we get together with friends that makes tea drinking so much fun.

PAR~TEA

AND NOW THERE ARE PAR-TEAS!

This *Totally Tea~rific Tea Party Book* celebrates tea-drinking customs, and some new activities of our own concocting. Find out what the southern belle says if her teacup takes a tumble, or how to suck a sugar lump like a true Russian. There is so much more to tea parties than drinking tea, and your party can take place almost anywhere. Don't worry if you can't supply the most perfect table settings and costumes; food and festivities are the most important things. From Boston cream pie to clover cookies, you will find recipes for all kinds of treats, along with heaps of activities for added "flavor." Learn to dance the Kazatsky, turn brooms into teepees, make food into face masks, and fashion hoola hoops into hoop skirts.

Or toss some tea bags and start a revolution!

First, put the kettle on. It's time for tea!

TEA~rific Tea

HOW TO PREPARE HOT TEA

1 cup (237 ml) cold water per person, plus 1 cup (237 ml) for the pot
1 heaping teaspoon (5 ml) tea leaves or 1 tea bag per person

Bring a kettle of water to a gentle boil over medium heat. Pour a cup of the hot water
into the teapot. Put the lid on the teapot and hold it down while you swish the hot water around.
Swish lightly, so you don't slosh any out of the spout! Pour the water out. This tea-making tradition
helps to keep the teapot hot. 🍃 Spoon out tea leaves or toss the tea bags into the warmed pot and
pour in hot water. Let the tea steep for 4 to 5 minutes. If you used loose tea leaves, pour the tea into
cups through a strainer. If you used tea bags, remove them.

HOW TO PREPARE COLD TEA

4 cups (or 1 liter) hot or cold water, depending on recipe
5 heaping teaspoons (25 ml) tea leaves or 5 tea bags per person
Additional ingredients, as desired
Water, juice, or soft drinks
Ice, crushed or cubed
Sweeteners
Lemon juice and slices
Mint or other decoration

Making cold tea is as simple as one, two, three.
First, prepare the tea very strong; second, dilute it a
little or a lot; and, three, chill it until it makes your teeth snap.
Most of the cold tea recipes found here follow this formula.

What's in a Teaspoon?

1 teaspoon = 1/3 tablespoon
3 teaspoons = 1 tablespoon
2 tablespoons = 1 ounce = 1/8 cup
4 tablespoons = 2 ounces = 1/4 cup
8 tablespoons = 4 ounces = 1/2 cup
16 tablespoons = 8 ounces = 1 cup
12 ounces = 1 1/2 cups
16 ounces = 2 cups

1 liter = 1,000 milliliters
237 milliliters = 1 cup
29.56 milliliters = 1 ounce
15 milliliters = 1 tablespoon
5 milliliters = 1 teaspoon

Be a Smar~TEA

About Brewing

BOILING WATER   Under medium heat, water comes to a gentle boil, and makes "soft" rolling bubbles. When water is heated under high heat, it comes to a "hard" boil, and all you see are moving bubbles.

LOOSE TEA   Loose tea comes in cans and bags. It is usually not finely ground, but is broken-up leaves, flowers, or stems. Put loose tea in a pot to steep, or use a tea strainer to make a single cup. Tea stays fresh for a long time when stored in a container with a tight lid.

STEEPING   Steeping is another word for soaking. The term is almost always applied to tea leaves or tea bags that have been placed in hot water. You watch the pot or cup until the tea water is as dark as you want it.

TEA STRAINERS   Tea strainers let hot water reach loose tea, but don't let the tea escape into the cup or pot. There's the little mesh cup with a handle that fits on a cup rim. And there's the one that's the shape of a small egg with holes in it that's called a tea ball.

TYPES OF TEA   Tea leaves all come from the same plant but make six main types of tea, depending on how they are processed: black, oolong, green, yellow, white, and flower-scented. There are also flavored teas, like lemon or cinnamon.

About Cooking

BEATING   Beating is using a fast up-over-down-and-around motion with a spoon, or using a beater. The results depend on how much liquid there is, from frothy bubbles to stiff peaks.

CREAMING   Creaming is getting a soft ingredient like butter to mix with a liquid ingredient like milk. You slowly add the liquid to the soft one and stir like crazy.

CUTTING/BLENDING   To get a dry ingredient like sugar to mix with a soft one like butter, you add the dry one a little at a time to the soft one.

DRY INGREDIENTS   Dry ingredients have no liquid in them, nor are they stiff. They are things like flour, sugar, baking powder, and soda.

MELTING CHOCOLATE   These days, the easiest way to melt chocolate is in a microwave. Use medium power in an uncovered dish. Stir every 15 seconds until the chocolate is shiny and smooth.

WET INGREDIENTS   Wet ingredients include anything that's slippery, gooey, or slimy, like milk, eggs, and butter.

Safe~TEA TIPS

Here are some ideas for keeping your tea parties happy affairs. It's no fun at all if you burn or cut yourself, spill stuff that stains the carpet, or make a huge mess. The common-sense tips that follow should help prevent anything TEA-rrible from spoiling your special event.

When you're planning...

When you're deciding what kind of tea party to have and inviting your friends, also make sure you include an adult in your plans. She or he should not only know what you're doing, but also be close by at all times.

When you're cooking...

Stay in the mood of the tea party and think civilized. Wear an apron, organize your ingredients and utensils before you start, wash your hands, and tie back any long hair. Chop slowly and carefully, have potholders ready, and do not walk away from anything cooking on top of the stove or in the oven. Most important, stay calm and cheery while you cook – the food will taste even better when you're done.

When you're crafting...

When you're painting, dyeing, cutting, sewing, stapling, or paper folding, pick a "safe" workspace, where it's okay to make a mess. Just in case spills happen, set out newspapers or an old sheet. The best way to avoid accidents is to work slowly and carefully.

When you're moving...

As you dance, stretch, or throw tea, be sure there's plenty of space to move around in, so that nothing breaks or falls down on you when you start to rumble. When working with sticks for playing miniature golf or making teepees, think about who is next to you. Tea parties should never include whacking of any kind, accidental or otherwise.

When you're drinking tea...

All kinds of tea, especially varieties of black tea and even some herbal teas, contain caffeine. Caffeine is called a stimulant because it can make you jumpy and leave you wide awake long after bedtime. So take care not to drink too much tea at one time. Most teas come in a decaffeinated form, so you won't have to stop drinking after one cup.

When you're par~TEAing...

Remember, pinkies raised, napkins in laps, and pleasant smiles are the essence of tea partying in style. But most of all, tea parties are for having *TEA~rific* fun!

THE *English* TEA PARTY

Whether they are too cold, too hot, too tired, or too excited, the British turn to a good old cup of tea. They prefer tea to most other beverages, and they like to drink it in style.

Official tea time is late afternoon. As the hostess, it is your responsibility to pour the tea and pass the cups to your guests, asking, "Milk or lemon? One lump of sugar or two?" Once everybody has been served, start making polite conversation, preferably about the weather or other topics that won't create too much of a stir. Have fun with your best English accent, extend your pinky out gracefully when sipping, and fill in any awkward silences with expressions like "Pip, pip!" and "By jove!" Scones served with butter or clotted cream and jam, crustless finger sandwiches made with finely sliced cucumber and watercress, and tea biscuits are traditional English tea goodies. Burp on an emergency basis only, and if you should have an accident with a finger sandwich, hide the evidence quickly under a napkin. (By the way, "finger" is a size, not an ingredient!)

WHAT TO WEAR

In Victorian times, afternoon tea was a social occasion. Even a special dress – the tea gown – was worn. Dress up for your English Tea Party in whatever makes you feel elegant – white gloves, a flowery or straw hat, shiny shoes, or a long dress. Tuck a lacy handkerchief into a glove to dab at your brow if it gets warm. Think graceful and posh, and don't forget your umbrella if you are having tea outside.

SETTING THE TABLE

 Pick a good spot to spend time talking, drinking tea, and eating goodies. Set up a table and chairs.

 Spread a lace tablecloth and put a white or floral-print napkin to the left of each place. Set a china cup on a saucer with a spoon to the right. Put a small plate and knife in the middle.

 When it's time for tea, place the teapot on a tray or trivet. A small pitcher of milk, a bowl with sugar lumps, and lemon wedges should be within easy reach.

Place a paper doily on a plate, and arrange the scones on top. Set out small china bowls containing the butter or clotted cream (or cream cheese) and strawberry jam.

ON THE menu

TASTE-TEAS

ENGLISH BREAKFAST TEA WITH MILK OR LEMON AND SUGAR

SCONES WITH BUTTER OR CLOTTED CREAM AND JAM

ACTIVI-TEAS

PAINTING UMBRELLAS

English Breakfast Tea

English breakfast tea isn't just for starting the day. It's a pick-me-up at any time. A hardy brew with a strong flavor, this tea is a blend of different types of black tea.

1 teaspoon (5 ml) English Breakfast tea leaves or 1 tea bag per person
Milk or lemon wedges
Lumps of sugar

Prepare as directed for hot tea (see page 8). Add plenty of milk. For a tart taste, instead, add lemon juice. For sweetening, try 2 to 3 lumps or teaspoons (10-15 ml each) of sugar.

Scones with Butter or Clotted Cream and Jam

Scones are the perfect companion for English breakfast tea. Serve with butter or clotted cream (cream cheese is a good substitute) and really good strawberry jam. Makes about 8 scones.

2 cups (473 ml) all-purpose flour
4 tablespoons (60 ml) plus 1 tablespoon (15 ml) granulated sugar
1 teaspoon (5 ml) baking powder
1/2 teaspoon (2.5 ml) baking soda
1/4 teaspoon (1 ml) salt

4 tablespoons (60 ml) butter
1/4 cup (59 ml) currants (optional)
1 1/2 cups (355 ml) plus 1 tablespoon (15 ml) cream
2-inch-wide (5 cm) cookie cutter
Clotted cream and strawberry jam for spreading

Preheat oven to 425°. 🍃 Sift the flour, 4 tablespoons (60 ml) of the sugar, baking powder, baking soda, and salt into a large mixing bowl. 🍃 Using a pastry blender or two dull knives, cut the butter into the flour mixture until the butter pieces are the size of small peas. 🍃 Optional: Stir in the currants. 🍃 Pour in the 1 1/2 cups (355 ml) of cream and mix until blended. 🍃 Put the dough onto a lightly floured work surface and knead for 1 minute, or until the dough is one big, smooth lump. Add more flour as needed to keep the dough from sticking. 🍃 Flatten the dough with a rolling pin until the dough is about an inch (2.5 cm) thick. Cut with a cookie cutter. 🍃 Place scones on a cookie sheet and brush with the remaining 1 tablespoon (15 ml) of cream. Sprinkle with sugar. 🍃 Bake for 15 minutes. Remove the cookie sheet from the oven with potholders. Using a spatula, transfer the scones to a wire rack to cool slightly before serving.
🍃 Let your guests spread on as much topping as they like.

PAINTING UMBRELLAS

Perhaps where you live it only rains for a while in the winter and spring. But imagine if it rained almost every day. The people who live in the British Isles spend a lot of time looking at the sky and wondering if it's going to rain. In fact, umbrella stands in many homes are filled with random umbrellas that people have left behind. Here's a great opportunity to make a unique umbrella that stands out as well as keeps the rain off.

NECESSI-TEAS

UMBRELLAS
ACRYLIC PAINTS

Get cheap, solid-colored umbrellas and paint designs on them with acrylic paints. Try flowers, plants, polka dots. ◎ Acrylics dry to a tough plastic, so your designs won't come off, even in a downpour. They won't wash off clothes, either, so paint carefully. ◎ Be cheery and zany, so that even when it's raining, you'll think bright, sunny thoughts.

The Teddy-Bear Tea Party

Teddy bears may be best known for their wild picnics in the woods, but every now and then they like to settle down to a fine cup of tea. After all, they deserve it. They are always there when you need a furry shoulder to cry on or a soft paw to squeeze. Invite your friends to bring along their favorite bear and give the teddies a tea to remember.

Bears have large appetites, so be sure to feed them plenty of their favorite foods. Honey and other sticky treats are always a big hit. But beware! Bears can be very greedy. If you want to share in the snacks, don't leave your guests unattended, even for a moment.

Once they have eaten, the bears will be full of energy for their favorite activities. They may want to act out their favorite play with an all-teddy cast, or show off their talents at a Super Bear pageant. If they are too full to move, they might even agree to sit still while you paint their very own bear portrait.

What to Wear

Put on something that is soft and comfortable, and you can feel squooshy like a teddy bear, too. If you like, wear all brown and pretend to be a big grizzly. After all, not all bears are the affectionate, fuzzy type.

Setting the Table

 Spread a low table with a soft, cotton tablecloth, and surround it with big, comfy cushions and pillows. Or you may want to have your party on the floor or rug, much like bears do in the woods.

 Set out colorful mugs and teaspoons, along with a pitcher of milk and a pot of honey. When the tea is ready, put the pot on a mat where everyone can reach it.

 Fill a big plate with Spiced Teddy-Bear Cookies (no fair grabbing).

On The menu

Taste-TEAS

Cinnamon Tea with Milk and Honey

Spiced Teddy-Bear Cookies

Activi-TEA

A Super Bear Pageant

CINNAMON TEA

Cinnamon is one of the oldest known spices to both human and bear. Cinnamon mixed with black tea makes a naturally sweet beverage with a delicious spicy aroma.

1 teaspoon (5 ml) cinnamon-flavored tea leaves or 1 tea bag per person, or a black tea of your choice with cinnamon stick or powdered cinnamon
Milk and honey

Prepare as directed for hot tea (see page 8). If you are adding the cinnamon flavor to the tea, one method is to put a cinnamon stick in the teapot and let it steep with the tea. Another method is to sprinkle powdered cinnamon on top of the hot tea after you have poured it. Add lots of milk – and honey, of course.

SPICED TEDDY-BEAR COOKIES

Like most teddy bears, these cookies are cute and warm. Don't let that stop you from gobbling them up. Makes about 1 dozen cookies.

1 1/2 cups (355 ml) all-purpose flour
1 teaspoon (5 ml) ground ginger
1/2 teaspoon (2.5 ml) ground cinnamon
1/4 teaspoon (1 ml) ground nutmeg
1/4 teaspoon (1 ml) salt
1/4 teaspoon (1 ml) baking soda
6 tablespoons (90 ml) butter, softened
1/4 cup (59 ml) firmly packed brown sugar
1 egg
1/4 cup (59 ml) molasses
Teddy bear-shaped cookie cutter
Currants (optional)

Sift the flour, spices, salt, and baking soda into a large mixing bowl, and set aside. ❧ In another smaller bowl, use a wooden spoon to cream the butter and sugar. Beat in the egg, followed by the molasses. ❧ Add the wet stuff to the dry stuff and mix until blended. ❧ Put the dough onto a piece of waxed paper. Using the palm of your hand, press the dough into a square about an inch (2.5 cm) thick. Wrap it in the waxed paper and refrigerate for 30 minutes. ❧ Preheat oven to 400°. ❧ On a floured work surface, use a rolling pin to roll the dough to 1/4 inch (.6 cm) thick. Add more flour as needed to keep the dough from sticking. ❧ Press the cookie cutter into the dough and transfer the teddy-bear shapes onto a cookie sheet. Gather the dough scraps into a ball and flatten them with the palm of your hand. Continue rerolling the dough and cutting more cookies until the cookie sheet is full. ❧ Optional: Push two currants into each cookie for eyes, and add another one below for a nose. ❧ Bake cookies for 10 minutes. Remove the cookie sheet with potholders. Using a spatula, transfer the cookies to a wire rack to cool.

A SUPER BEAR PAGEANT

Even teddy bears like to play dress-up once in a while. After you invite them to your tea party, you might suggest some post-tea "dolling up," and see if they're in the mood. Make sure they aren't feeling too competitive about who is going to be Super Bear, and remind them that the real fun is being the cuddliest and all-around nicest bear they can be.

Gather all your bears and clothes together – doll clothes, baby clothes, your clothes, and outfits from grown-ups' closets (get permission). Don't forget shoes, jewelry, scarves, ties. Other accessories like ribbons, sunglasses, or handbags can strongly sway the judges. ◎ Points should also be given for poise, congeniality (how nice she or he is to the other bears), and best entertainment act. ◎ Once you've picked the winner, dress her or him up as Super Bear. Get something red to be the robe. Cut out a crown from cardboard and staple it together, painting it if you like. Make a scepter by wrapping a wooden spoon with aluminum foil and tying some ribbons to the bottom. ◎ Now, dressed like a star, Super Teddy can do a slow march to the tune of "Here she/he comes, Bear America . . ."

NECESSI-TEAS

TEDDY BEARS

CLOTHES AND SHOES OF ALL KINDS

JEWELRY, SCARVES, AND BAGS

OPTIONAL: WOODEN SPOON, ALUMINUM FOIL, AND RIBBONS

THE *TEE* PARTY

For those whose golf terminology is rusty, the tee is a small peg that sits in the ground and holds the golf ball in place as the golfer takes a stroke (swing). It is the starting place for each hole to be played and, in this case, the starting point for a terrific tea party.

Golf is one of the most civilized sports, so it is only fitting to celebrate it with a civilized beverage – a cup of tea, of course. Golfers do a lot of walking, swinging, and bending as they play, so they work up quite an appetite. Be sure to prepare plenty of snacks and enough cold tea for a hot day in the sun.

Show you are serious about golf by dropping a few references to sand traps, fairways, and woods and irons. Before you know it, you will be teeing the ball like a young Tiger Woods and TEA-ing like a pro, as well.

WHAT TO WEAR

Serious golfers have to be prepared for all kinds of weather, so they usually go for a layered look with shirts, vests, and zippered jackets. More casual golfers have also been known to sport some interesting plaid combinations, so feel free to put on whatever puts you in a swinging mood.

Gloves – golfing or biking ones – give a good grip on the "iron," as well as a professional look. Any color will do! Sunglasses and sunscreen are obvious golfer necessities.

SETTING THE TABLE

 Set a card table or picnic table outside, preferably on a lawn. Or forget the table altogether, and take tea on the green.

 Put a small plate holding a Teecake with Green Frosting at each guest's place, along with a paper napkin and a large glass filled with ice and a straw.

In the center of the spread place a big pitcher or bowl of Sun Tea and a plate of extra cakes.

ON THE *menu*

TASTE-TEAS

SUN TEA OVER ICE

TEECAKES WITH GREEN FROSTING

ACTIVI-TEA

MAKING A MINIATURE GOLF COURSE

Sun Tea

Sun tea is an American invention that brews, as you might suspect, in the heat of the sun. Makes about 1 dozen large glasses.

8 cups (or 2 liters) cold water
8 tea bags black tea
8–16 teaspoons (40-80 ml)
    granulated sugar

Combine water and tea bags in a pitcher or glass bowl. Cover the top with plastic wrap, so no critters will get in. Set it outside in the sun and let the tea bags steep for 3 or so hours. Add water or ice if the tea looks too strong. Add more tea bags if the tea looks too weak, or wait a little longer for the sun to do its magic. Stir in 1 to 2 teaspoons (5-10 ml) of sugar for each cup of tea just before serving. Serve nature's concoction over ice.

Teecakes with Green Frosting

Just in case you don't have a bright green putting lawn, these cakes will give you the feeling that you do. Makes about 8 cakes.

Ingredients for Teecakes
2 medium-sized carrots
3/4 cup (178 ml) all-purpose flour
1/2 cup (118 ml) granulated sugar
1 teaspoon (5 ml) baking powder
1/2 teaspoon (2.5 ml) cinnamon
1/2 teaspoon (2.5 ml) allspice
1/4 teaspoon (1 ml) salt
1/3 cup (79 ml) vegetable oil
1 egg
2 tablespoons (30 ml) lemon juice

Ingredients for Green Frosting
1 cup (8 oz, 237 ml)
    cream cheese
1/4 cup (59 ml) butter,
    at room temperature
1 1/2 cups (355 ml) powdered sugar
1 teaspoon (5 ml) vanilla
1 teaspoon (5 ml) green food coloring
8 mini-marshmallows (optional)
8 toothpicks with flags (optional)

Preheat oven to 350°. Line an 8-cup muffin tin with cupcake papers. ❧ Wash the carrots and cut off the ends, then use a vegetable peeler to take off the skin. ❧ Grate the carrots medium fine with a vegetable grater. Be careful not to grate your fingers! ❧ Sift all the dry ingredients into a large bowl. ❧ In a smaller bowl, mix the oil, eggs, grated carrots, and lemon juice until blended. ❧ Add the wet mixture to the dry mixture and mix until blended. ❧ Fill the muffin cups 3/4 full. Bake teecakes for 20 minutes. Remove the muffin tin with potholders and let cool. ❧ Make the frosting while the cakes are cooling. In a large bowl, mix together all the frosting ingredients. Spread the frosting on the cooled cupcakes. ❧ Optional: For a ball-and-flag effect, insert a festive toothpick into a mini-marshmallow and push it into the top of each cake.

MAKING A MINIATURE GOLF COURSE

U nlike regular golf, miniature golf is great because you can play it anywhere, make your own course, and create your own rules. Whoever gets the ball in the most holes wins. So start teeing off!

NECESSI-TEAS

OPEN SPACE

BROOMSTICKS OR GOLF CLUBS

GOLF BALLS

CUPS OR BUCKETS

OPTIONAL: CLOTHES HANGERS, BOXES, PAINTS, STUFFED ANIMALS, BIRD BATH

To make your own golf course, all you need is a lawn or any outdoor or indoor area where you can roll some balls. ◎ Place some cups or buckets on their sides, and use broomsticks or golf clubs to hit golf balls into them. ◎ Plan your course. Decide where you will begin to tee off and where your course will end. ◎ Use the terrain to make challenges – hills, curves, distances. ◎ Add obstacles to make the game harder. Put the hook on a clothes hanger into the ground and shoot the ball through the triangle. Use the sides of a box as a tunnel. You can paint it to look like a whale's mouth or an intergalactic highway. ◎ Make your course into a theme park. Pretend dirt patches are moon craters and make a space walk. Or create a circus stroll by placing your stuffed animals in strategic places. ◎ Incorporate what's already in the garden – use a bird bath for a hole-in-one. Just make sure no birds are taking a bath! The more creative you are with your course, the more fun you will have.

THE *Chinese* TEA PARTY

Legend has it that tea was discovered by a Chinese emperor almost 5,000 years ago when a tea leaf accidentally blew into a pot of boiling water. Today China has the largest variety of tea anywhere in the world, and the Chinese people drink tea all day, every day – at home, in teahouses, and in restaurants.

The Chinese do not have a complicated tea ceremony like the Japanese, but they do take their tea drinking seriously. Proper manners are all important, so remember these simple rules: Greet your guests with a nod or a slight bow. If you go for the bow, bend from the waist and look toward the ground, then follow up with a gentle handshake, if you wish. Never use a person's first name unless you are invited to do so. Instead, refer to them by their title: princess, doctor, master tea brewer. Lastly, do not boast, even if you are a princess, do not giggle or get overly excited, and do not forget to drink plenty of China's best brew.

WHAT TO WEAR

Dress elegantly in soft fabric, preferably a colorful silk dress. Traditional Chinese dresses are long, and have high necks, short sleeves, and slits up the sides. If you don't have a dress like this, wear anything with geometric patterns or pictures of animals and plants. Green, red, black, white, and yellow are the ancient colors worn by emperors and officials.

SETTING THE TABLE

 Surround a low table with flat, colorful pillows. Hint: The Chinese believe that the color red brings good fortune.

 Decorate the table with traditional Chinese china, which is often blue and white, but comes in many beautiful colors and designs. Bright red ribbons, prints of Chinese calligraphy, or a shallow bowl filled with floating flowers and leaves can add to the festive mood.

 Set each place with Chinese teacups, which are small and have no handles, or little bowls. Put small saucers nearby, perhaps decorated with dragons, along with red napkins.

 Use a clay or stoneware teapot, placed next to a tray filled with fortune cookies.

ON THE menu

TASTE-TEAS

OOLONG TEA

FORTUNE COOKIES

ACTIVI-TEA

FORTUNE WRITING

OOLONG TEA

Oolong is one of the six main types of tea, all made from the same tea plant but processed differently. (Others include white, green, and black teas.) Most oolong tea comes from China and Taiwan. It has a light, fresh flavor, and is usually drunk plain, with no added milk, sugar, or lemon.

1 heaping teaspoon (5 ml)
   oolong tea leaves or
   1 tea bag per person

Prepare as directed for hot tea (see page 8). Usually, there's no need to sweeten.

FORTUNE COOKIES

Although the Chinese have a strong tradition of believing in things that bring good fortune, fortune cookies actually originated in California. Ever since Edward Louie, of the Lotus Fortune Cookie Company in San Francisco, devised a clever folding machine for the cookies, they have become a happy custom in Chinese restaurants all over the United States, and in China as well. Makes about 1 dozen cookies.

2 egg whites
1 teaspoon (5 ml) vanilla extract
1/4 teaspoon (1 ml) salt
1/2 cup (118 ml) all-purpose flour

1/2 cup (118 ml) granulated sugar
Strips of paper with fortunes
   written on them in ink

Preheat oven to 400°. 🌿 Set an empty egg carton, a small bowl, and the fortunes nearby. 🌿 Line a cookie sheet with lightly greased foil. 🌿 Lightly whisk the egg whites and vanilla extract. Add the flour, sugar, and salt. Whisk vigorously until the mixture is runny. 🌿 Spoon a few teaspoons of dough onto the cookie sheet. Using the back of the teaspoon, swirl each blob of batter into a circle 3 inches (7.5 cm) wide. 🌿 Bake the cookies for 5 minutes, or until they have turned golden around the edges. Remove the cookie sheet from the oven using potholders. 🌿 MOVING QUICKLY, remove each cookie with a spatula and place upside down on a work surface. Lay a fortune across the middle and fold the cookie in half. Careful, it's hot! Pick up the cookie by the corners and drape it over the edge of the small bowl, pulling down on the corners to create the shape of a fortune cookie. Place each shaped cookie, points down, into an egg-carton cup until cool. 🌿 Prepare one cookie sheet while the other is baking to help the process move faster.

FORTUNE WRITING

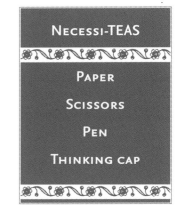

Wake up your ancient wisdom and write it down! Write funny fortunes, too, like, "Confucius say, 'Too many cookies upset stomach.'"

NECESSI-TEAS

PAPER

SCISSORS

PEN

THINKING CAP

When you sit down to write fortunes to go in your cookies, you can go with such classics as, "You will soon go on a long trip" and "Good fortune will come to you." ◎ You can make up your own, too. Just spend a minute gazing into your mental crystal ball and reading the future for your friends. You might write, for example, "The boy you like will ask you out" or "Work hard and you will get good grades." ◎ You can also use fortunes as an opportunity to tell something to a friend, such as, "You are a good friend" or "Loose lips sink ships." ◎ Cut small rectangles of paper, then write out your fortunes in ink, ready to tuck into the cookies. Let random luck or fate(!) carry the right message to the right gal.

The Mad Hats Tea Party

When the Mad Hatter came to Alice in Wonderland's tea party, he created a stir even before he took a sip of tea. Now it's your turn to turn heads with a mad hat of your own.

Hats have been around throughout the ages, keeping out the sun, showing kingly greatness, hiding magicians' rabbits, or simply looking spectacular. Whether it's a beret or a bonnet, a top hat or a giant sombrero, the hat has a way of making a bold statement about who you are and all the important things you are off to do.

The Mad Hats Tea Party is a chance for you and your friends to go a little crazy and design the hats of your wildest dreams. Get as colorful as you can, as tall as you wish, and parade about grandly.

WHAT TO WEAR

Y our new hat, of course, and whatever colorful, silly clothes you may have. Clothes that are too big or someone else's are also fun to wear (get permission first).

ON THE

TASTE-TEAS

BLACKBERRY TEA WITH HONEY

PEANUT BUTTER AND CHOCOLATE SWIRLS

ACTIVI-TEA

HAT DECORATING

SETTING THE TABLE

 Spread a tablecloth designed with bright colors and a wild pattern. Set each place with mismatched cups and saucers or mugs.

 See if you can find a fun, wacky-looking teapot. Try to give everyone a different style of napkin and a small plate.

 Find a large plate for the swirl cookies and place it in the center of the table.

Blackberry Tea

This tea comes from a blackberry bush. It makes a tea that is tart, tangy, and juicy sweet.

1 heaping teaspoon (5 ml)
    loose blackberry tea
    or 1 tea bag per person
Honey

Prepare as directed for hot tea (see page 8). Sweeten with a spoonful of honey.

Peanut Butter and Chocolate Swirls

These cookies are so good they would convince the maddest hatter to sit down and sip some tea. Makes about 16 cookies.

1 cup (237 ml) all-purpose flour
1/4 teaspoon (1 ml) baking powder
1/4 teaspoon (1 ml) salt
4 tablespoons (60 ml) butter,
    at room temperature

1/2 cup (118 ml) firmly packed brown sugar
1 egg
1/3 cup (79 ml) smooth peanut butter
1 cup (6 ounces, 180 ml) chocolate chips
1 tablespoon (15 ml) water

In a large bowl, sift the flour, baking powder, and salt. In a medium-sized bowl, cream the butter and sugar. Add the egg and peanut butter, and mix until blended. Add the peanut butter mixture to the flour mixture and mix until blended. Remove half of the dough into a separate bowl and set aside. Put chocolate chips in a plastic or glass bowl and put in a microwave oven on medium heat for 30 seconds, then stir. Continue heating and stirring until melted, 15 seconds each time. Mix the chocolate into one of the bowls of dough until blended. Dump each bowl of dough onto a separate sheet of waxed paper. Use the palm of your hand to form the dough into a square about 1/4 inch (.6 cm) thick. Brush the chocolate square with water. Place the plain dough on top of the chocolate dough, pressing down to secure. Roll the dough into the shape of a tube. Wrap it in waxed paper and refrigerate for 30 minutes. Preheat the oven to 350°. Slice the rolled dough into 1/4-inch (.6-cm) rounds and place them on a cookie sheet. Bake the cookies for 12 minutes. Remove the cookie sheet from the oven with potholders. Using a spatula, transfer the cookies to a wire rack to cool.

HAT DECORATING

Decide whether or not you want to make a new hat or dress up one you already have. Ask your head, "What do you feel like today?" and see what it says.

See what decorations you have around the house. If you're going to make a new hat, get out cardboard or felt and use a stapler or needle and thread. Imagine how high you want the hat to go, then measure around your head, leaving extra material for the seam. (Be sure to have many conversations with your head as you go, so that you appear appropriately mad.) Cut the top down, if you need to, and cut a round piece to fit over the top. If you want to make a brim, make it like a donut so it's open where you put your head in. Now for the really fun part: decorating your hat, new or old, with drawn designs or lettering, buttons, beads, stickers, even fresh flowers – whatever strikes your fancy.

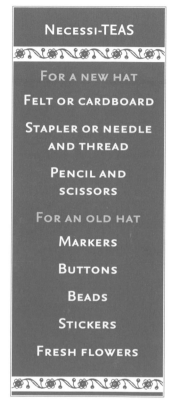

NECESSI-TEAS

FOR A NEW HAT

FELT OR CARDBOARD

STAPLER OR NEEDLE AND THREAD

PENCIL AND SCISSORS

FOR AN OLD HAT

MARKERS

BUTTONS

BEADS

STICKERS

FRESH FLOWERS

THE INDIAN TEA PARTY

India is one of the largest producers of tea in the world, and tea in its various forms is very much the favorite drink among locals. Sometimes it is served English style from an elegant teapot. More often, though, you will find numerous chaya, or street teas, being boiled in an open kettle, served in small clay cups, and mixed with lots of milk, sugar, and spices.

Indian people enjoy savory foods with their tea, so be sure to have a hearty spread. When it is time to eat, turn to each of your guests and form a pyramid shape with your hands. This is a traditional greeting showing that it's time for the party to begin. Close your eyes, imagine the heat and color of a far-away tropical port, and dig into some rare treats.

WHAT TO WEAR

A sari is the traditional dress of Indian women. To wear it properly, first put on a short-sleeved blouse and a slip or a thin skirt. Find a piece of silk or cotton with bright colors and beautiful designs. To make it into a sari, first wrap the cloth around your hips, tucking the top end into the slip. Then bring the rest of the material up under your right arm and over your left shoulder, so that it falls at knee level. Wear sandals and, if you like, use lipstick, eye shadow, or eye liner to make a bindi. A bindi is traditionally a red dot worn by Hindus on the forehead between the eyes. This spot is known as the third eye.

SETTING THE TABLE

 Dress up the table with layers of shimmery silk or decorative material in golds, pinks, yellows, greens, and blues. You can even put up a picture of the Taj Mahal!

 Set the tea sandwiches, served on a shiny plate with a serving fork, in the center of the spread, along with a fancy teapot. Scatter flower petals all over the table.

Put a cup and saucer at each place. Each guest should also have a colorful napkin and a small plate.

ON THE menu

TASTE-TEAS

CHAI

TEA SANDWICHES WITH YELLOW CURRY AND MANGO CHUTNEY

ACTIVI-TEA

HENNA TATTOOING

CHAI

Chai (rhymes with pie) is the word for tea in many parts of the world. Chai from India is usually made starting with a base of black tea and whole milk. It's the spices and sugar that make it so special.

4 cups (or 1 liter) cold water

4 sticks cinnamon

6 whole cloves

2-inch (5-cm) piece of fresh ginger, cut into pieces

6 whole cardamom pods (optional)

1 cup (237 ml) whole milk

4 heaping teaspoons (20 ml) loose black tea

1/3 cup (79 ml) granulated sugar

Combine the water and spices in a saucepan. Boil for 5 minutes over medium heat. Turn the heat to low. Add the milk, tea, and sugar and simmer. Remove chai from the stove, cover, and let steep for 5 minutes. Pour through a tea strainer into mugs and serve.

TEA SANDWICHES

Both yellow curry and sweet mango chutney are flavors of India. They taste wonderful together with spicy chai. Makes 16 finger sandwiches from 4 regular ones.

1/2 cup (118 ml) butter, softened

1/4 teaspoon (1 ml) yellow curry

1 teaspoon (5 ml) granulated sugar

1/3 cup (79 ml) sweet mango chutney

8 slices finely textured bread

In a small bowl, mix the butter, curry, and sugar until blended. ❦ Spread a thin layer of curry butter on half of the bread slices. ❦ Spread a thin layer of chutney on the remaining slices and form the sandwiches. ❦ Carefully trim off crusts with a sharp knife. ❦ For finger sandwiches, cut each sandwich square into four long rectangles or triangles. Or make many different shapes by using cookie cutters to cut the sandwiches.

HENNA TATTOOING

Henna comes from crushed leaves from the henna plant, and is commonly used to decorate hands and feet at Indian weddings and other ceremonies. With henna tattooing, you get to paint each other or yourself. It doesn't hurt, and the reddish brown color lasts 1 to 4 weeks. You'll want to make the mix before your party because it has to sit for at least 6 hours before you can use it.

2–3 bags black tea
2–3 tablespoons (30–45 ml) whole cloves
Juice of 1 lime or lemon, or juice from concentrate
3 tablespoons (45 ml) henna powder – the best is green, not yellow
     (check the Internet or Indian grocery stores)
Lemon sugar – juice of half a lemon mixed with
     1 tablespoon (15 ml) sugar (optional)

NECESSI-TEAS

PLASTIC SPOON AND CERAMIC BOWL

PLASTIC WRAP

APPLICATOR – THE BEST IS A LITTLE SQUIRT BOTTLE WITH A METAL TIP, AS USED WITH FABRIC DYES (LOOK IN ART OR FABRIC STORES)

Put 1 cup (237 ml) of water in a saucepan, and add the tea and cloves. At this point, you can add any other herbs you like, for more color or a wonderful smell. Boil until you have 1/2 cup (118 ml) of liquid. Strain and set aside. ◎ Juice the lime or lemon and strain out the pulp. Or use prepared juice. ◎ Put the henna in a small ceramic bowl. With a plastic spoon, add the juice, then slowly add most of the tea mixture and stir until it is the consistency of toothpaste. Set aside the tea that is left. ◎ Cover the henna mix with plastic wrap, put it in a dark place, and let it sit for at least 6 hours. It will not be strong enough otherwise. It must be used in the next 24 hours or it will not stain effectively. ◎ Just before applying, slowly add the rest of the tea mixture, rewetting the henna with the tea so that it is soft (like toothpaste) and will squirt out of the applicator. ◎ Henna painting is easiest to apply on hands and feet, and ankles and wrists, but can be done anywhere on the body. The henna should stay on for 1 to 6 hours. ◎ Optional: After application, put some lemon sugar on the henna to help it stick.

THE *SOUTHERN BELLE* TEA PARTY

Southern belles are well known for throwing the best parties. Even on all those hot afternoons, they manage to stay free of sweat and to treat their guests to the grandest of get togethers. This includes the tea party, which the belle makes extra-fancy with linen napkins, silver spoons, and sparkling conversation.

Even more important than the fine table settings and refreshing drinks is behaving like a southern lady. At all times, the belle is sweet, charming, and very witty. Wait graciously on all your guests, and if you should get overexcited and spill tea on your frock, twist your parasol and utter something that Scarlett O'Hara would say, like, "Oh, fiddlededee!" or "I'll think about that tomorrow." But today, try your own hand at southern hospitality with a tasteful tea party of your own.

WHAT TO WEAR

Wear a hoop skirt, a long skirt and fancy top, or a ruffled dress. You may want to wear light colors to stay cooler in the sun. Don't forget to bring an umbrella to protect your skin from the hot southern rays.

ON THE
menu

TASTE-TEAS

LEMON ICED TEA WITH MINT

FIDDLELESS FUDGE

ACTIVI-TEA

MAKING HOOP SKIRTS

SETTING THE TABLE

 Try to have your Southern Belle Tea Party outside on a lovely patio or under the shade of a backyard tree or table umbrella.

 Spread a linen tablecloth on the table, and set each place with a tall glass filled with ice and adorned with a sprig of mint. Each guest should also have a small plate, a dainty napkin, and a silver dessert fork.

 Arrange the fudge on a cakestand or crystal or glass plate. Set it in the center of the table next to a large pitcher of iced tea dressed up with lemon slices and more sprigs of mint.

Lemon Iced Tea

Iced tea was invented in 1904 by a clever Englishman at the St. Louis World Fair. He was trying to introduce Indian tea to Americans, but in the stifling weather he was getting few takers. After he dropped some ice cubes into the brew, thirsty people came flocking and iced tea was born. Makes 5 to 6 glasses.

4 cups (or 1 liter) cold water
5 heaping teaspoons (25 ml) loose
    black tea or 5 tea bags
1/4 cup (1 ml) granulated sugar
4 cups (.95 liter) lemonade,
    made from concentrate
Ice cubes and sprigs of mint

Prepare the tea as directed for hot tea (see page 8). Add the sugar to the tea and stir. Let cool. Fill a pitcher with ice. Pour in the lemonade and tea, mix, and serve. Use a tea strainer for loose tea leaves. Add mint and more ice, if desired.

Fiddleless Fudge

Scarlett might want to impress her friends with her great-tasting fudge, but don't for a minute think she'd spend much time making it. She'd have loved this recipe, which is fudge, only faster. Makes about 1 dozen fudge pieces.

1/2 cup (118 ml) heavy cream
2 teaspoons (10 ml) vanilla extract
4 cups (.95 liter) powdered sugar
1/4 teaspoon (1 ml) salt

4 ounces (120 ml) unsweetened chocolate
1 tablespoon (15 ml) butter
1 cup (237 ml) chopped walnuts (optional)

Oil an 8 x 8-inch pan. ✺ In a large bowl, mix the cream, vanilla extract, powdered sugar, and salt until blended. ✺ Break up the bar of chocolate into a nonmetal bowl and add the butter. Put in a microwave oven on medium to high heat for 30 seconds, then stir. Continue heating and stirring until melted, 15 seconds each time. ✺ Add the hot liquid to the sugar mixture and mix vigorously until combined. Optional: Stir in the walnuts. ✺ Spread the fudge mixture in the oiled pan and refrigerate for 30 minutes. ✺ Cut into squares and serve.

MAKING HOOP SKIRTS

Bring back the Old South as it was 150 years ago by recreating your version of the hoop skirt. When you put on a dress that is really big at the bottom, it's as if you turn into a swan, in this case, a southern swan. So put on your southern twang, too.

Get out your hoola hoop; a belt; some yarn, string, or rope; and either a sheet (look for a colored one) or a big swatch of fabric. ◎ Put on the belt and tie at least 4 lengths of string to it – all around you – back, side, and front, cutting the strings where they touch the floor. ◎ Tie the strings to the hoola hoop at about ankle height. ◎ Drape a sheet or fabric over the hoop and around your waist, tucking the top into the belt. ◎ Optional: For a more permanent skirt, you can finish the bottom with stitches, sewing the hoola hoop into a hem. Otherwise, staple it, or pin it (ask permission).

NECESSI-TEAS

HOOLA HOOP

BELT

STRING, ROPE, OR YARN

SHEET OR FABRIC

NEEDLE AND THREAD, STAPLER, PINS (OPTIONAL)

THE *TEA* BALL

By the turn of the last century, "tea dancing" had become all the fashion. Women would wear "tea gowns" to eat, drink tea, and be merry. In keeping with this tradition, the Tea Ball is a perfect occasion to dress up, eat and drink up, and dance until dawn (or at least until dinner).

Balls often have a theme. You might have a Snow Ball to announce the coming of winter or a BaseBall during baseball season. This, of course, is a Tea Ball, to celebrate tea. But you could, for example, have a Masquerade Tea Ball, if you are feeling adventurous.

Even if you don't spy any princes at your ball, you never know when one might show up. You might even consider inviting some princes, or boys. Be prepared and dress appropriately. Wear your most dazzling gown, your shiniest jewels, and some ballet slippers for easy gliding across the floor. When you have had your tea, take the hand of the person sitting next to you and ask kindly if you "may have the pleasure of the next dance."

WHAT TO WEAR

To do the tango, wear a dress that shows a little shoulder. Put on your dancing shoes or sandals with heels, and place a single carnation between your teeth or in your hair. If boys have not been invited, lead dancers may want to dress up in boys' clothes.

SETTING THE TABLE

 Push the table against the wall, so that you'll have room to dance. The table should be arranged so that your guests can mingle around the drinks and snacks before being whisked off to the dance floor.

 Cover the table with a shimmering or lace tablecloth. Arrange a centerpiece of beautiful flowers. If the Tea Ball has a theme, add some props to the table setting; for a Masquerade Ball, for example, you'd add face masks.

Surround a punch bowl with punch glasses and cocktail napkins. Don't forget the ladle, so that your guests can serve themselves. Arrange the gourmet snacks on a few plates and set them around the table.

ON THE
menu

TASTE-TEAS

TEA PUNCH WITH MINT AND ICE

CHOCOLATE-COVERED FRUIT

ACTIVI-TEA

DANCING THE TANGO

TEA PUNCH

First concocted in France in 1653, tea punch has become a popular beverage all over the world. Punch is typically made with lemon, sugar, and fruit juice, but there are any number of tasty variations to this festive drink. Makes 12 servings.

Crushed ice
4 cups (or 1 liter) cold water
5 heaping teaspoons (25 ml) loose
    black tea or 5 tea bags
4 cups (.95 liter) cranberry juice
4 cups (.95 liter) ginger ale
Sprigs of mint and ice cubes

Prepare the tea as directed for hot tea (see page 8). Fill a punch bowl with ice. Pour in the tea. Pour the tea through a tea strainer if you used loose tea leaves. Add the juice and ginger ale, and stir. Ladle the punch into ice-filled cups garnished with a mint sprig.

CHOCOLATE-COVERED FRUIT

Why shouldn't your food be as dressed up as you for this fancy ball? Makes enough sauce for 6 to 8 servings of fruit.

Suggested Fruits

Strawberries, with stems on
Tangerine sections
Dried banana circles
Dried apricot halves
Dried pineapple rings, cut in half

Ingredient for Sauce

2 cups (12 oz, .36 liter) semi-sweet chocolate chips

Line a cookie sheet with waxed paper. Prepare any combination of fruit and set aside on the sheet of waxed paper. 🍃 Put the chocolate chips into a plastic or glass bowl. Put into a microwave oven on medium heat for 15 seconds, then stir. Continue heating and stirring until melted, for 15 seconds each time. 🍃 Dip the fruit in the liquid chocolate to cover 3/4 of each piece. Remicrowave briefly if the chocolate becomes too cool to coat the fruit. 🍃 Lay the chocolate-dipped fruit on waxed paper and refrigerate for a few minutes, until cool.

DANCING THE TANGO

The tango is a passionate dance with pizzazz. Find some tango music and go cheek-to-cheek stepping sideways across the room. Count it out as you move your feet to the tango beat.

Stand facing each other. The "lead" leads; the "follow" mirrors the lead and shouldn't think too much about which foot is moving right or left. ◎ The lead goes left foot forward (slow), right foot forward (slow), then left foot forward again (quick), right foot forward again (quick). Finally, the left toe just touches the right foot (slow), then the left foot begins the step pattern all over again. ◎ The follow does the same steps, only opposite. ◎ Lead and follow move side by side, holding hands with arms outstretched. When they get to the end of a room, they quickly turn around, switch hands and feet, and go off in another direction. Ta da!

> ### NECESSI-TEAS
>
> **TWO PEOPLE**
>
> **TANGO MUSIC (ASK AN ADULT)**
>
> **SPACE TO MOVE ACROSS A FLOOR**

THE *BOSTON* TEA PARTY

The Boston Tea Party is "steeped" in history. In 1773, the English forced their extra tea onto the American colonies by sending three tea ships from the East India Company to Boston. Angered by this attempt to control their market, colonists decided to rebel. A band of patriots disguised themselves as Mohawks, attacked the tea chests with axes, and emptied 342 of them into the water. The Boston Tea Party was one of the main events that led to the American Revolution. Three years later, after several more "tea parties" and other historic happenings, America was triumphant and the Declaration of Independence was signed.

For a while, Americans stayed away from tea because it seemed too English. However, they could not resist the leaf for long, and today Americans drink more tea than ever before. Make your Boston Tea Party a time to be festive. Prepare a hardy brew, serve heaps of food, and remember to celebrate the Land of Freedom with a good show of red, white, and blue.

WHAT TO WEAR

Be patriotic! Dress up in red, white, and blue, or be revolutionary and reenact what people wore during the actual Boston Tea Party. Red Coats should wear red jackets, if possible. The pretend Mohawks should walk in moccasins or go barefoot, wear leather skirts and halter tops, and braid their hair.

SETTING THE TABLE

 To celebrate America's independent spirit, decorate the table with as much red, white, and blue as possible. Fly an American flag above the table or just outside the window.

 Set each place with an individual cake, along with a dessert fork, teaspoon, napkin, cup, and saucer.

 Arrange the teapot, pitcher of milk, and bowl of sugar in the center of the table.

ON THE menu

TASTE-TEAS

DARJEELING TEA SERVED WITH MILK AND SUGAR

BOSTON CREAM PIE

ACTIVI-TEA

A REVOLUTIONARY TEA-BAG TOSS

Darjeeling Tea

Darjeeling tea is grown in Sri Lanka. Its popularity around the world means there's every possibility it was one of the teas landing in Boston Harbor. It is rich-tasting and flavorful, and a beautiful golden color.

1 heaping teaspoon (5 ml)
  Darjeeling tea leaves or
  1 tea bag per person
Milk and sugar (optional)

Prepare tea as directed for hot tea (see page 8). Add milk and sugar if desired.

Boston Cream Pie

This is the strangest pie you'll ever see. That's because this historical dessert is really a cake. Makes at least 8 cakes of pie.

1 frozen pound cake
2 1/4 cups (18 oz, 532 ml) prepared vanilla pudding
1/2 container (8 oz, 237 ml) prepared chocolate frosting

Cut the cake into 1/2-inch (1.25-cm) slices (2 slices per person). ❧ Spread 1/4 cup (2 oz, 59 ml) of the pudding on half of the slices. ❧ Cover the remaining slices with chocolate frosting. ❧ Place the frosting-covered slices, frosting side up, on the pudding-covered slices. ❧ Serve as individual cakes.

A REVOLUTIONARY TEA-BAG TOSS

It's time to throw some tea around. Do you want to be a British Red Coat or an American colonist dressed up as a Mohawk? Divide and conquer!

NECESSI-TEAS

TEA BAGS

BUCKET

Put a bucket in the middle of the room. Each side should stand in a circle around it, far enough away so that it's not too easy to toss tea bags in. Ready, set, go! ☺ The Red Coats should go first; when they throw their tea bags, they are bringing bales of tea into the Boston Harbor. Give them thick English accents and have them act very properly as they march to their spots. See how many tea bags they manage to land in the bucket. ☺ Then let the pretend Mohawks have their go as they throw their bales of tea into the Boston Harbor (bucket). Count how many bags they were able to dump, and declare one side the winner. ☺ To make the next round harder, use markers on the floor and move farther back. ☺ Toss as many times as you like; winner keeps all – the tea!

THE *TEEPEE* PARTY

The Native American teepee is an impressive sight to behold, not to mention an ingenious twist on home design. Teepees were used by tribes living on the Great Plains of today's United States and Canada. Always on the move hunting for buffalo, their dwellings had to be durable, quick to build, and easy to carry. Covered in animal skins, teepees kept their inhabitants warm in winter and cool in summer, and took women only a few minutes to pack onto a horse.

As first-time teepee builders, it might take you and your guests a little longer to build your shelter. However, it is well worth the effort. For a small tea party, a teepee is the perfect gathering place for private chats, cozy storytelling, or secret activities. It's also a good spot to hide teatime treats from hungry parents, not to mention roaming buffalo.

WHAT TO WEAR

Go barefoot or wear moccasins, if you have them; and braid your hair. Beads were once used as money and still play an important part in Native American ritual clothing. Beads also make good decorations, either sewn onto a garment or worn as a necklace.

ON THE menu

TASTE-TEAS

SMOKY TEA

CORN MUFFINS WITH BUTTER AND JAM

ACTIVI-TEA

BUILDING A TEEPEE

SETTING THE TABLE

 Spread a towel or blanket on the floor inside the teepee. Collect some small bowls or mugs to drink the tea from, and set them in the middle of the teepee.

 Sit in a circle around the teapot, bowls or mugs, and muffins. Invite your guests to serve themselves.

 Serve the corn muffins from a woven basket lined with a cloth napkin.

SMOKY TEA

Tea leaves destined to become smoky teas are prepared in a special way. They are rolled and dried over smoking pine fires, giving the final brew its distinct smoky smell and flavor.

1 heaping teaspoon (5 ml)
    Lapsang souchong tea leaves
    or 1 tea bag per person

Prepare as directed for hot tea (see page 8). Smoky Tea is so flavorful, nothing needs to be added.

CORN MUFFINS

Native tribes from all over the Americas appreciate the many ways to cook with corn – also called maize. Try your own hand at a corn confection. Makes 8 muffins.

1 cup (237 ml) yellow corn meal
1 cup (237 ml) all-purpose flour
1/3 cup (79 ml) granulated sugar
1 1/2 teaspoons (7.5 ml) baking
    powder
1 teaspoon (5 ml) baking soda

3/4 teaspoon (4 ml) salt
1 cup (237 ml) sour cream
1/4 cup (59 ml) milk
2 eggs
4 tablespoons (60 ml) melted butter
Butter and jam

Preheat oven to 425°. 🌿 Line an 8-cup muffin tin with cupcake papers. 🌿 In a large bowl, sift together all the dry ingredients, then set aside. 🌿 In a medium-sized bowl, blend the sour cream, milk, eggs, corn, and butter. 🌿 Combine the wet mixture with the dry mixture, just until blended. 🌿 Spoon batter into the lined muffin tin to 3/4 full. 🌿 Bake muffins for 20 minutes. Take the muffin tin from the oven using potholders, and let cool. 🌿 Remove the muffins from the tin and serve with butter and jam.

BUILDING A TEEPEE

What do you get when you take a stack of sticks and stand them all up together? A teepee. Teepees are amazing houses. You'll be making one very similar to the real thing, only a whole lot smaller – unless you have very long poles on hand.

NECESSI-TEAS

4–7 BROOMS

MARKERS OR PAINT (OPTIONAL)

Have each of your friends bring over a broom or two. A teepee can have as many as seven, but needs at least four. ◎ Lean the brooms together with the brush end down. Remember to leave two of them far enough apart to make an entrance. ◎ Tie the brooms together at the top with rope, so they stay put. ◎ Wrap a sheet around the outside; secure one end by weaving it behind one of the doorway brooms and in front of the one next to it. The sheet on the opposite side of the doorway becomes the door flap. ◎ Optional: If you have permission, you may want to paint the sheet with simple shapes or designs, like triangles and lines, suns and moons, or feathers.

THE *IRISH* TEA PARTY

Set the mood for your Irish Tea Party by getting out your finest green linens. Ireland is a green land and green has long been associated with its favorite holiday, St. Patrick's Day, and its national emblem, the three-leafed clover, called a shamrock. (Four-leafed clovers are quite rare and very lucky!) In case you don't take this matter seriously, let it be known that school children in Ireland have developed a nasty tradition of pinching anyone who doesn't wear green on St. Patrick's Day.

The Irish are very superstitious, especially when it comes to teatime. Be sure to stir your tea clockwise unless you want to anger the spirits. Also, keep an eye out for a wrinkly elf called a leprechaun. It won't drink too much tea because it is exceedingly small, but seeing one guarantees to bring you a lifetime of good fortune.

WHAT TO WEAR

Green is the most obvious color to wear in this Irish party. You could also wear a pretty, long dress and some clover sprigs and green ribbons in your hair.

SETTING THE TABLE

 Spread a lace or linen tablecloth, preferably green.

 Set each place with a china cup and saucer, spoon, small plate, and green napkin.

 In the center of the table set a green plate of shamrock-shaped cookies, the teapot, pitcher of milk, and sugar bowl.

 Arrange a tiny vase of clovers picked from your yard, and wish your guests luck in finding one with four leaves.

ON THE menu

TASTE-TEAS

IRISH BREAKFAST TEA, PERHAPS WITH MILK AND SUGAR

GREEN CLOVER COOKIES

ACTIVI-TEA

PAINTING POTS AND PLANTING SHAMROCKS

Irish Breakfast Tea

Rumor has it that the Irish consume more tea than any other nationality, including the English. To battle those cold, blustery days, they take their tea dark and strong. Most Irish tea blends fit this description.

1 heaping teaspoon (5 ml)
    Irish breakfast tea leaves or
    1 tea bag per person
Milk and sugar (optional)

Prepare as directed for hot tea (see page 8). In Ireland, tea is often served plain, but can also be enjoyed with milk and sugar.

Green Clover Cookies

Want to have good luck? Then chow down on some of these tasty clovers. Makes about 16 cookies.

1 cup (237 ml) all-purpose flour
1/4 teaspoon (1 ml) salt
1/4 teaspoon (1 ml) baking powder
4 tablespoons (60 ml) butter, softened
1/2 cup (118 ml) granulated sugar
1 egg

1/2 teaspoon (2.5 ml) vanilla extract
1/2 teaspoon (2.5 ml) green food
    coloring
Clover cookie cutter
Green sprinkles

In a large bowl, sift the flour, salt, and baking powder, and set aside. In a medium-sized bowl, cream the butter and sugar with a wooden spoon. Beat in the egg, food coloring, and vanilla extract. Add the butter and sugar mixture to the flour mixture and mix until blended. Place the dough on a sheet of waxed paper. Use the palm of your hand to form the dough into a square about 1 inch (2.5 cm) thick. Wrap in waxed paper and refrigerate for 30 minutes. Preheat oven to 400°. On a floured work surface, use a rolling pin to roll the dough to 1/4 inch (.6 cm) thick. Add flour as needed to keep the dough from sticking. Press the cookie cutter into the dough to form the cookies, and set the cookies aside. Reroll the dough scraps and cut into more cookies. Put the green sprinkles on top of the cookies. Using a wide spatula, transfer them to a cookie sheet. Bake cookies for 10 minutes. Remove the cookie sheet from the oven using potholders. Using a spatula, transfer the cookies to a wire rack to cool. Try not to get too lucky by eating these cookies all at once!

PAINTING POTS AND PLANTING SHAMROCKS

I t's great to be green – in every sense of the word! Wearing it and growing it and eating it. Get back to earth by sitting down with a terracotta pot and some paints, and thinking about the beautiful images you see in nature.

Put some scrap paper or newspaper on a table, and have everyone sit around the table and paint. Decorate your pot with some favorite designs; use some razzle-dazzle or go for calm beauty. ◎ Hunt up some clover seeds and get them started in your pretty pot. If you don't want to wait for the seeds to sprout, just buy some small plants to place in the pots. ◎ To stay in an Irish mood, play some lively jig music while you paint and pot.

NECESSI-TEAS

TERRACOTTA POTS

PAINTS

CLOVER OR OTHER SEEDS

IRISH MUSIC

THE RUSSIAN TEA PARTY

Russians consider tea a national beverage. They drink it all day long, keeping it warm with a clever and beautiful invention called the samovar. Strong tea is brewed in a little pot that sits on top of the samovar and then diluted with hot water that comes from a tap on the side. In addition to making the room cosy, the samovar can provide enough tea for up to forty unexpected visitors!

If you don't have a samovar for your tea party, you can still impress your friends with Russian tea-drinking traditions. Russians don't usually take milk with

their tea, although they like the flavor of lemon. Having a bit of a sweet tooth, they like to mix their tea with a spoonful of jam or a cube of sugar. The jam you can stir into the tea or eat straight from a plate, taking sips of tea between mouthfuls. The sugar cube you can hold firmly between your teeth for a hint of sweetness while drinking. Should you have difficulty with the sugar trick and make unusual throaty noises, just explain that you are making a toast, in Russian.

WHAT TO WEAR

The Kazatsky is traditionally a man's dance, so you'll want to dress up like one to do the dance. But not like any man – wear a long shirt and let it hang over your pants, then tie a rope belt around your waist. Everything should be baggy. Finish your outfit with some hefty boots.

SETTING THE TABLE

 Decorate the table with a paisley tablecloth or embroidered, fringed shawls and tall candlesticks.

Russians generally use glass cups with metal handles. If you can't find those, set each place with china cups and saucers, a dessert plate and fork, a napkin, and a teaspoon.

In the center of the table place the plate of blintzes, the teapot or samovar, a bowl of jam, a stack of sugar cubes, and a plate of sliced lemons.

ON THE
menu

TASTE-TEAS

RUSSIAN CARAVAN TEA WITH LEMON, SUGAR CUBES OR JAM

CHEESE BLINTZES

ACTIVI-TEA

DANCING THE KAZATSKY

RUSSIAN CARAVAN TEA

Russian caravan tea is made from a blend of black and oolong teas. It gets its name from the long caravan, containing up to three hundred camels, that used to carry tea from China to the Russian nobility.

1 heaping teaspoon (5 ml)
Russian caravan tea leaves
or 1 tea bag per person
Lemon slices or wedges
Sugar cubes and jam

Prepare as directed for hot tea (see page 8). Let your guests decide if they want to add lemon, sugar, or sweet jam – or any combination of the three!

CHEESE BLINTZES

It may take a few tries, but once you get the hang of it, blintzes (a type of crepe) are really easy to make. Makes 8 blintzes.

Ingredients for Blintzes
1 1/4 cups (296 ml) all-purpose flour
1/4 teaspoon (1 ml) salt
1 cup (237 ml) milk
3 eggs
4 tablespoons (60 ml) butter, melted

Ingredients for Filling
3 cups (710 ml) ricotta cheese
6 teaspoons (30 ml) granulated sugar
1 lemon for drizzling
Powdered sugar for sprinkling

Combine all blintz ingredients in a blender and blend until smooth. Pour the mixture into a bowl. 🍃 Heat a large, nonstick skillet over a medium-high flame. Spray the pan with nonstick cooking spray. 🍃 When the pan is hot, pour 1/4 cup (59 ml) of the batter into the pan. Swirl the batter to form a thin layer by tilting the skillet in a circular motion. 🍃 Cook for 2 to 4 minutes, until the edges start to curl slightly. 🍃 Using a wide spatula, flip the blintz. Cook for another 1 to 2 minutes. 🍃 Remove the blintz from the pan using a spatula. Lay blintzes on top of each other on a plate next to the stove. 🍃 To make the filling, mix ricotta cheese and sugar in a medium-sized bowl. 🍃 Spread a spoonful of filling into the center of each blintz. Fold the sides in onto the filling to form a square. Turn over onto a plate. 🍃 Squeeze with lemon juice and sprinkle with powdered sugar. 🍃 Blintzes go well with fruit, apple sauce, and strawberry jam.

DANCING THE KAZATSKY

You have probably heard of the Kazatsky. It's an old Russian folk dance, and has a habit of showing up in movies, and even in cartoons.

This is the dance where you bend your knees so you're resting on your heels, and then kick one leg out at a time with your foot straight up. You may fall over – it's very hard on your thighs – so feel free to unfold your arms and hold on to something, the floor or the wall or a friend, so you can keep your balance. ◎ Make sure that when you kick out each leg you say, "Hey!" and that you are very high-spirited. ◎ Practice is over. Time for you and your friends to try doing it together, all in a line with your arms woven together and holding onto each other's shoulders. This helps the dancers keep their balance, but being linked together means that everyone can fall over all at once, too!

NECESSI-TEAS

RUSSIAN DANCE MUSIC

STAMINA!

THE T-SHIRT PARTY

It's time to celebrate the American T. You probably have a bundle of them nestled on the floor of your closet, but when did you last think of honoring them with their very own party?

The humble T-shirt became an official word in the American English dictionary in the 1920s; by World War II it had become standard underwear for the Army and Navy. Whether it is keeping our troops comfy, our top halves cozy, or making a bold statement on Ricky Martin's chest, the mighty T never fails to please.

Wear one of your favorites to the T-Shirt Party and bring a plain one along for a T-shirt makeover. You will have a tie-dye to die for and a tip-top T for any occasion.

WHAT TO WEAR

Wear your tie-dye shirts when they're dry, but until then go for the brightest colors you've got. Primary colors and stripes are great, a bunch of them together. Throw on a bright vest, too!

ON THE

TASTE-TEAS:
HIBISCUS TEA
MARBLE MUFFINS

ACTIVI-TEA:
TIE-DYEING T-SHIRTS

SETTING THE TABLE

 Spread a bright cotton tablecloth. Set each place with colorful mugs, small plates, and fun napkins.

 Put your jazziest teapot and a large plate of the muffins in the center of the table.

 Decorate the wall with a tribute to your favorite T-shirt-toting stars.

HIBISCUS TEA

Made from brilliant red flowers, this tea should put you in a colorful mood. It has an exotic spicy flavor and a rich ruby tone.

1 hibiscus flower tea bag
   per person

Prepare the tea bags as directed for the leaves in hot tea (see page 8). This tea is so light and refreshing that it requires no diluting or sweetening.

MARBLE MUFFINS

These crazy muffins are almost as colorful as your T's will be. Makes 8 muffins.

1 box lemon cake mix (you may need water,
   eggs, and oil for this – be sure to check the box!)
1 tablespoon (15 ml) red food coloring
1 tablespoon (15 ml) blue food coloring

Preheat oven to 375°. Line an 8-cup muffin tin with cupcake papers. Make the cake mix according to the package directions. Divide the batter in half into two bowls. Add one color of food coloring into each bowl and mix into the batter until blended. Add more food coloring until you get the color you want. Use 2 measuring cups or coffee mugs to pour both the colors of batter into a cupcake paper at the same time. The batters should be side by side in the cupcake cup. Create a marble effect by dragging a dull knife through the batter in a circular motion. Experiment to find the method and design you like. Bake muffins for 30 minutes. Remove the muffin tin from the oven using potholders, and let cool before digging in.

TIE-DYEING T-SHIRTS

This is a great activity for a sunny afternoon. You'll want to be outside because of the possible mess, and the colors are easier to see out there, too. The results are not instant, but tend to be spectacular!

You'll need to get a tie-dye kit or dyes from an arts and crafts store, and it's good to have old containers for mixing colors to paint onto your white shirts. Make sure your shirt is cotton. Prepare for dyeing by putting down plenty of newspapers and putting on rubber gloves – no need to make a huge mess or dye your hands. Fold the T in pleats like an accordion, and twist it. Tie it with string or rubber bands. Or twist sections into tubes. To get circles inside each other, tie each section with rubber bands in 3 or 4 places. When you are finished, soak the T in water and a dye fixer for 30 minutes or as instructed. Paint or squirt the colored dye on, in whatever patterns you like. Put the dyed shirt in a plastic bag overnight and untie it in the morning. Rinse it out, and wash it by itself in cold water.

NECESSI-TEAS

PLAIN WHITE COTTON T-SHIRTS

TIE-DYE KIT OR DYES, FIXER, AND BRUSHES

OLD CONTAINERS

NEWSPAPERS AND RUBBER GLOVES

STRING OR RUBBER BANDS

BRUSHES OR SQUIRT BOTTLE

PLASTIC BAGS

THE *BEAU~TEA* PARTY

Maybe your hair caught on fire in the chemistry lab. Maybe you have had an attack of the flu. Or maybe you just need to catch up with friends on the latest gossip. There are many good reasons for a Beau-Tea Party, not the least of which is the chance to play with your food.

You will soon discover that many foods that are good for your tummy, such as cucumber, yogurt, and tea, are just as good for your skin. As you treat your face to nature's lotions and potions, bathe your feet in a tub of warm water.

Breath deeply and rid your mind of all unimportant thoughts, except maybe what color nail polish to wear with your new rosy complexion. Prepare to look good enough to eat, and to see the contents of your refrigerator in a whole new light.

WHAT TO WEAR

To be in a beautifying mood, strip to the essentials (you), then get comfy in a terrycloth robe. A towel made into a turban will protect your hair. Wear soft slippers or go barefoot, in preparation for painting your toes. Make sure the room is warm enough so you can stay very relaxed. Follow your facial with a soothing bath or shower. Ahhhh.

SETTING THE TABLE

 Decorate the table with soothing, natural colors like mossy green or soft peach. Burn a nice-smelling candle and arrange some flowers in a vase.

 At each place set an earth-toned cup and saucer, small plate or bowl, fork, and cloth napkin.

 Serve the fruit salad from a big glass bowl in the center of the table, alongside a simple teapot.

 You may also want to have your tea in mugs in the bedroom, for sipping while you beautify.

ON THE
menu

TASTE-TEAS
MINT TEA
FRUIT SALAD

ACTIVI-TEA
GETTING A
FOOD FACIAL

MINT TEA

Herbal teas are made from the roots, stems, flowers, or leaves of various plants. Mint tea, made from mint leaves, has a clean, crisp, refreshing flavor.

1 tablespoon (15 ml) torn fresh or dried mint leaves or 1 tea bag per person

You may find mint in your own garden. Pick the leaves fresh or dry them for later use. Prepare as directed for hot tea (see page 8). Served light or dark, this tea needs nothing extra.

FRUIT SALAD

All this dazzling fruit will surely help to bring out your inner glow. Makes about 4 servings.

1/2 cup (118 ml) pineapple, cut into cubes
1/2 cup (118 ml) banana, cut into circles
1/2 cup (118 ml) apple, cut into wedges
1/2 cup (118 ml) nectarine, cut into wedges
1/2 cup (118 ml) green grapes
1/2 cup (118 ml) red grapes
1/2 cup (118 ml) raspberries
1/2 cup (118 ml) blueberries
3 tablespoons (45 ml) granulated sugar
1/3 cup (79 ml) orange juice
Yogurt and honey (optional)

Cut each of the fruits into bite-sized pieces. ❦ Combine cut fruit in a large bowl. ❦ Sprinkle with sugar and drizzle with fruit juice. Using two large spoons, toss the fruit in the bowl. ❦ Optional: If you have any yogurt and honey left over from your facials, try putting some on top of the fruit. Enjoy!

GETTING A FOOD FACIAL

ou've heard that "you are what you eat," right? Well, how about, "You are what you don't eat but put on your face instead?" Do you feel refreshed after you eat yogurt or honey or oatmeal? Every pore of your face will feel like that too, after applying a facial mask, made nature's way.

Mix up the ingredients for the facial. Rub the mixture gently onto your skin, avoiding your eyes. Or you may want one of your friends to put it on for you. ◎ Leave the facial mask on for 10 minutes. ◎ Optional: As you lie back to let the food do its magic, press sliced cucumber slices on your eyelids. Very relaxing. ◎ When time is up, throw the slices away and rinse off the mask with warm water. Prepare to feel soothed and smoothed.

NECESSI-TEAS

FOR EACH FACIAL

1 TABLESPOON (15 ML) PLAIN YOGURT

1 TABLESPOON (15 ML) HONEY

1 TABLESPOON (15 ML) CHAMOMILE TEA, COOLED

4 TABLESPOONS (60 ML) DRIED OATMEAL — ENOUGH TO MAKE A GOOD PASTE

2 CUCUMBER SLICES (OPTIONAL)

THE JAPANESE TEA PARTY

The Japanese "way of tea" or chado goes far beyond tea drinking as we know it. It actually trains people to reach enlightenment. No wonder the famous tea ceremony can go on for several hours and schooling in the art of the ceremony can take as many years.

Remember these four words when you are having your Japanese Tea Party: harmony, purity, respect, and tranquility. You may not reach the spiritual heights known to the great tea masters, but you will go a long way toward setting the right mood. The Japanese drink mostly green tea. Savor the taste and aroma as you sip it, think relaxing thoughts, and try to be graceful, even as you tackle your food with slippery chopsticks. You should know, though, that making slurpy sounds is not only acceptable but honorable, because it shows the cook that you are really enjoying the meal.

What to Wear

Sport a traditional Japanese robe, or kimono, if you have one. Otherwise, wear a silk dress or anything brightly colored with wide sleeves. Tie a wide cloth belt around your waist to look like the kimono sash or obi. As Japanese girls get older, the sash is worn lower and made narrower, so be mindful of how low you go. Sandals make good footwear to honor the Japanese custom of removing one's shoes before entering the house.

On The *menu*

Taste-TEAS
Green Tea
Vegetable Sushi

Activi-TEA
Making Origami Swans

Setting the Table

 Create a tranquil setting in a quiet room decorated with paper lanterns, bonsai trees, a vase with a single flower or some bamboo stalks, and maybe even a tiny fishbowl.

 Surround a low table with pillows or bamboo mats. Set each place with small bowls for the tea, small plates, and a pair of chopsticks.

 In the center of the table arrange a Japanese-style teapot, which sometimes has the handle on the top. Put the plate of sushi next to it.

 Decorate the table with origami swans.

GREEN TEA

Green tea is an acquired taste. If you're not immediately impressed by the flavor, you may be won over by its many supposed health benefits.

1 heaping teaspoon (5 ml) loose
    green tea leaves or 1 tea bag
    per person

Prepare as directed for hot tea (see page 8). Green tea should always be drunk plain.

VEGETABLE SUSHI

After making these sushi rolls, just sit back, digest, and meditate. Makes 12 to 15 sushi rolls.

1 cup (237 ml) white, short-grained rice
3 tablespoons (45 ml) rice vinegar
1 tablespoon (15 ml) sugar
1/2 teaspoon (2.5 ml) salt
1 cucumber
1 avocado, peeled, cored,
    and sliced into thin strips

1 package nori (dried sheets of seaweed)
Makisu (bamboo mat) or plastic wrap
    and cloth
Soy sauce
Chopsticks (optional)

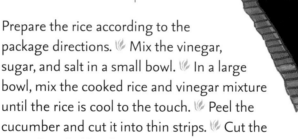

Prepare the rice according to the package directions. 🍵 Mix the vinegar, sugar, and salt in a small bowl. 🍵 In a large bowl, mix the cooked rice and vinegar mixture until the rice is cool to the touch. 🍵 Peel the cucumber and cut it into thin strips. 🍵 Cut the avocado in half and remove the pit and skin. Cut it into thin strips. 🍵 Place a sheet of nori on the makisu. Wet your fingers with clean water and spread a thin, even layer of the rice mixture on two-thirds of the nori sheet. 🍵 Place vegetables across the center of the rice mixture. 🍵 Dab some water along the edges of the nori to help seal it. Then roll the nori using the makisu to help form the shape of a tube. Squeeze the roll inside the makisu to seal the edge. 🍵 Cut the roll into six pieces using a sharp, clean, wet knife. Wipe the knife clean and rewet it after you cut a few slices. 🍵 If you don't have a makisu, try using plastic wrap on top of a cloth for rolling. 🍵 Use soy sauce for dipping as you eat. If chopsticks are too clumsy, use your fingers.

MAKING ORIGAMI SWANS

O rigami is a Japanese word meaning "to fold paper," and it's fun to see the figures emerge from a blank page.

You can make beautiful creatures out of any paper you find in your house. Just make sure that the sheet you're working with is square. Fancy paper is also available at any crafts store, shiny and with bright colors. ☺ Make your first creations with big pieces of paper, because it's easier to see what you're doing. Here are instructions for making a swan. Make lots of them and have a swan parade across the tea party table!

NECESSI-TEAS

PAPER

SCISSORS (TO MAKE YOUR PAPER SQUARE)

THE *NIGHT~TEA* PARTY

idnight feasts are very well and good, but who has the patience to wait until the witching hour? The Night-Tea Party, a fun twist on the traditional sleepover, can be held anytime after dark. What's more, because not everyone in the house is sound asleep, you can howl at the moon at the top of your lungs.

Depending on the mood, the Night - Tea Party can be snuggly or scary, a time to gaze at the stars or to summon spooky spirits. It's always a good occasion to tell mysterious tales of wandering woodsmen, with the lights dimmed and voices hushed. Whatever you do, though, keep a pot of chamomile tea close by. It will soothe the soul and bring rest to the rest of you!

WHAT TO WEAR

Wear pajamas or clothes with moons and stars or clouds and sky. If you don't happen to have those prints in your closet, go for straight black, and pin on something sparkly.

SETTING THE TABLE

 Spread a black tablecloth for the night, and fold white napkins to make you think of the moon. Lay the cloth on the floor or a coffee table, and light a few candles for stars. If you have any star ornaments or glow-in-the-dark galaxies, feature them in your setting.

 Arrange the Moon-and-Star Cookies on a dark plate so that the sprinkles will sparkle. Set each place with a mug and a small plate.

 Place the teapot and cookies in the center of the tablecloth.

ON THE
menu

TASTE-TEAS

CHAMOMILE TEA

MOON-AND-STAR COOKIES

ACTIVI-TEA

STAR GAZING

Chamomile Tea

Chamomile tea is made from a daisylike plant with white flowers, and contains special herbs that actually help you relax. It also has a strong, soothing smell, so you can find your cup even in the dark!

1 heaping tablespoon (15 ml)
    dried chamomile flowers or
    1 tea bag per person

Prepare the flowers as you would for the leaves in hot tea (see page 8). The taste and scent flowers are all that's needed.

Moon-and-Star Cookies

These cookies twinkle, thanks to the colorful sprinkles. They're perfect for eating on the blackest of nights or by the light of the moon. Makes about 16 cookies.

1 cup (237 ml) all-purpose flour
1/4 teaspoon (1 ml) salt
1/4 teaspoon (1 ml) baking powder
4 tablespoons (60 ml) butter,
    softened

1/2 cup (118 ml) granulated sugar
1 egg
1/2 teaspoon (2.5 ml) vanilla extract
Moon and star cookie cutters
Colored sprinkles

In a large bowl, sift the flour, salt, and baking powder, and set aside. In another bowl, cream the butter and sugar with a wooden spoon. Beat in the egg and vanilla extract. Add the butter and sugar mixture to the flour mixture and mix until blended. Place the dough on a sheet of waxed paper. Use the palm of your hand to form the dough into a square about 1 inch (2.5 cm) thick. Wrap and refrigerate for 30 minutes. Preheat the oven to 400°F. On a floured work surface, roll the dough to about 1/4 inch (.6 cm) thick. Add more flour as needed to keep the dough from sticking. Press cookie cutters into the dough to form cookies, and set the cookies aside. Reroll the dough scraps and cut again into more cookies. Apply the colored sprinkles. Using a wide spatula, transfer the cookies to a cookie sheet. Bake the cookies for 10 minutes. Remove the cookie sheet from the oven with potholders. Using a spatula, transfer the cookies to a wire rack to cool.

STAR GAZING

When you're lying flat and looking far out at the night sky, you can actually tell that gravity is the only thing holding you down. You're on a planet in space, looking across the galaxy!

Make sure you schedule star gazing for a time when the moon isn't too full or too bright, because the darker the sky, the more stars you'll see. Also, you're best off if this party is somewhere away from city lights. But most important of all is a clear sky, so know your weather. ☺ Check the newspaper or the Internet to see if any astronomical events are coming up, such as comets or night planets in the sky. There are special times of year for shooting stars, too (especially in early August), so if you star gaze then, you're bound to get a good show. ☺ There's always so much to see. Grab a book or map of the constellations, along with a flashlight, blankets, and pillows, and get cozy looking out into space.

NECESSI-TEAS
GOOD STAR-GAZING CONDITIONS
CONSTELLATION BOOK OR MAP
FLASHLIGHT
BLANKETS AND PILLOWS

Taste-TEAS

TEAS

Thanks goes to everyone who participated in the creation, direction, and production of this book. We couldn't have done it without all of you!

Creative Director
Hallie Warshaw

Lead Writer
Tanya Napier

Recipe Writer
Katrina Hendricks

Activity Writer
Lael Kimble

Graphic Designers
Tanya Napier
Hallie Warshaw
Madeleine Budnick

Photographer
Julie Brown

Illustrator
Annie Galvin

Editor
Robyn Brode

Production Artist
Doug Popovich

Photo Assistant
Phyllis Christopher

Photoshoot Assistants
Kris Bhat
Marcio Baggio

Special thanks to all the *TEA~rific* tea-party models:

Sarah Jane Allen
Taylor Allen
Carolyn L. E. Bazen
Surya Bhat
Dyantha Burton
Julia Burton
Olivia Byers-Straus
Maya Ruth Cameron
Kelly Rae Elmore
Zoe Ho Seher
Jenny McMillan
Gabrielle Rodriguez-Fusco
Franchesca Saulson
Perry Naimark Shadwick
Emiko Shimabukuro

Photoshoot Homes:
The Byers-Straus family
The Ho Seher family

Created and produced by **Orange Avenue Publishing, Inc.** 599 Third Street, Suite 306, San Francisco, CA 94107

ABOUT THE CREATORS

Tanya Napier is a writer, designer, and painter of teddy-bear portraits. She grew up in England, where she learned a good deal about tea and scones. She has written for various publications in Boston and New York, and now works as a copywriter and graphic designer in San Francisco. A graduate of Brown University, Tanya resides in Berkeley, California.

Tanya enjoys the occasional "cuppa." She takes her tea with milk and sugar.

Julie Brown enjoys photographing people – their lives and surroundings. One of her specialties is black-and-white documentary photography. Her photographs have been featured in various local and national publications, and this is her third children's book. Julie holds a Bachelor of Fine Arts from the Rochester Institute of Technology. She lives in San Francisco.

One of Julie's favorite ways to unwind is with a warm cup of peppermint tea.

Annie Galvin can't decide if she's an illustrator who writes or a writer who illustrates. Making paper dolls and writing poems are a few of her favorite pastimes. Originally from Ireland, Annie lives in San Francisco with her husband, a painter who writes.

Loyal to her homeland tradition, Annie enjoys a good strong cup of Irish tea in the afternoon.

Hallie Warshaw loves children's books, bright colors, and dogs. Her book ideas are inspired by her eccentric and talented southern Grandma Fanye, fun and creative childhood birthday parties, and summers as an arts-and-crafts counselor at Lake Farm Camp in Cape Cod.

Before founding Orange Avenue Publishing in 1997, Hallie was a creative director and graphic designer in Hong Kong, Osaka, and New York. She holds bachelor degrees from Clark University and the Rhode Island School of Design. She lives in San Francisco in a pastel blue building that she wishes were bright orange.

Hallie has always been a tea devo-TEA – she drinks it almost every day in almost every way.